Billy Wants a Blue Whale

Written and illustrated by
Cudd L Fish

I would like to dedicate this book to the most special
people in my life:

Kailo, Hunter, Aries, Nate, Jacob, Avery,
Zachery, Markus, Erikson, Raina, Anika
and Benzen,
This book is for you guys.

A very special thanks to my beautiful wife
and all my family and friends.

ave you ever heard of a blue whale?

I have seen one with my very own two eyes.
They are one of the most magnificent
and mysterious animals on the planet.
However,
this is not just a story about blue whales,
rather a story about a young boy named Billy
who simply adored them....

Billy always sat in his favorite spot up on the hillside
watching the blue whales off in the distance,
blowing their water spouts high in the air.
Young Billy loved watching the blue whales so much,
all he could ever think about was blue whales.
They were always on his mind.

"When I grow up I'm going to get a blue whale."
Billy would say to anyone who would listen.
There was just one problem....
Owning a blue whale was no easy task.
Some details would prove to be a tad bit complicated.
Billy seemed to think otherwise.
He thought a blue whale would make the perfect pet.
Billy was going to get himself a blue whale!

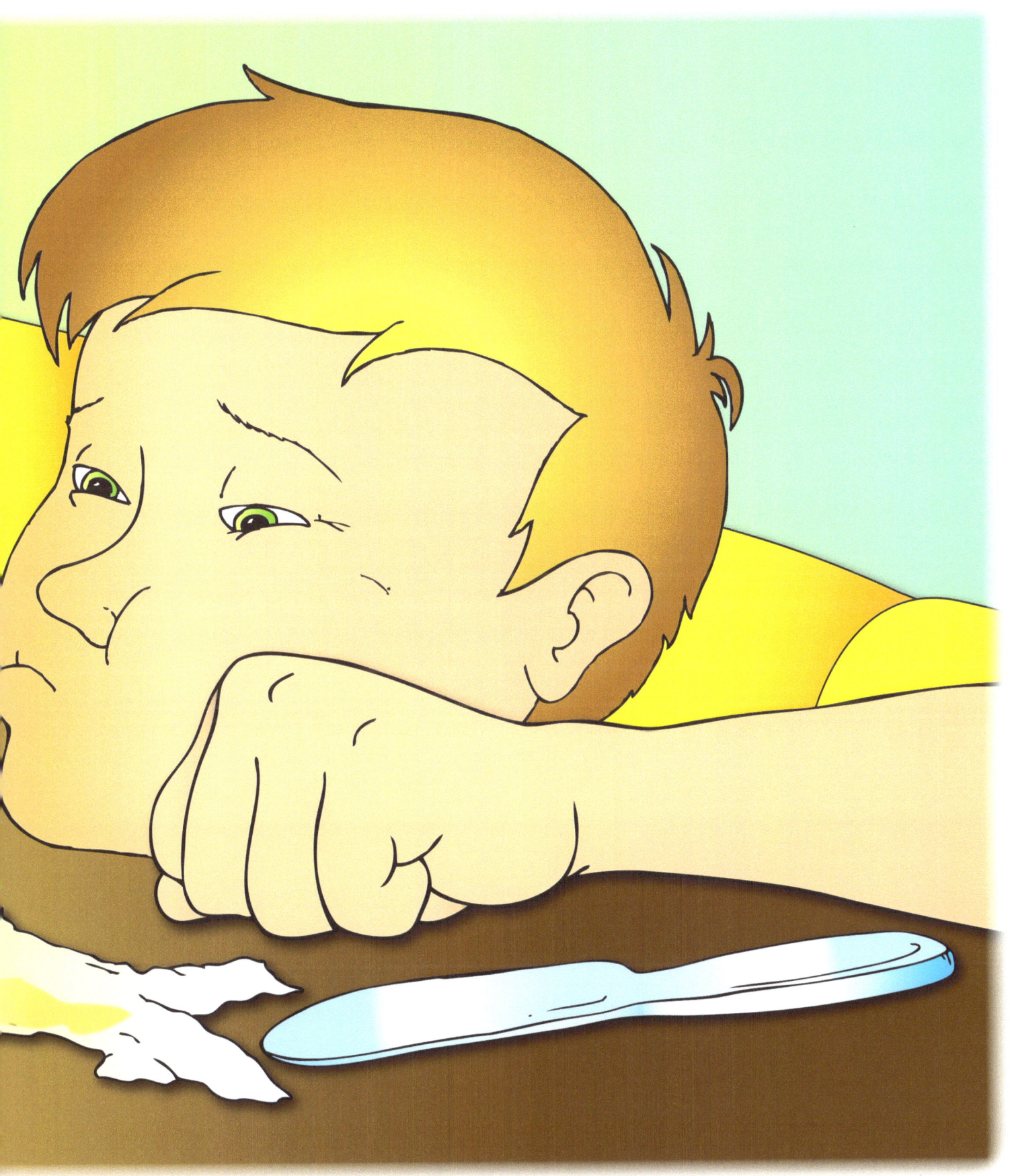

One day when Billy was chatting with his older brother,
he decided to tell him about his master plan.
"Did you know that when I grow up I am going to get a blue whale?"
Billy said, clearly catching is brother off guard.
"How will you get him home Billy?" His brother chuckled as he replied.
"Piece of cake!" Billy responded. "I will pull him home with my shiny red wagon."
He was going to get himself a blue whale, no doubt about that.

"Well I have a news flash for you Billy."
His brother said with a smirk.
"A blue whale can weigh as much as 26 full grown elephants."
"I don't think your little red wagon could handle such a task Billy."
"Wow," he replied. They didn't look quite that big from his perch up on the hill.
Never the less, Billy wanted a blue whale.

"What will you feed him?" Billy's brother asked.
"I am going to feed him cheeseburgers
and pepperoni pizza." Billy confidently replied.
"No no no." Said Billy's older brother.
"As tasty as that sounds, it would never work."
"Blue whales prefer to eat tiny crustaceans
called krill, and they eat tons of them!"

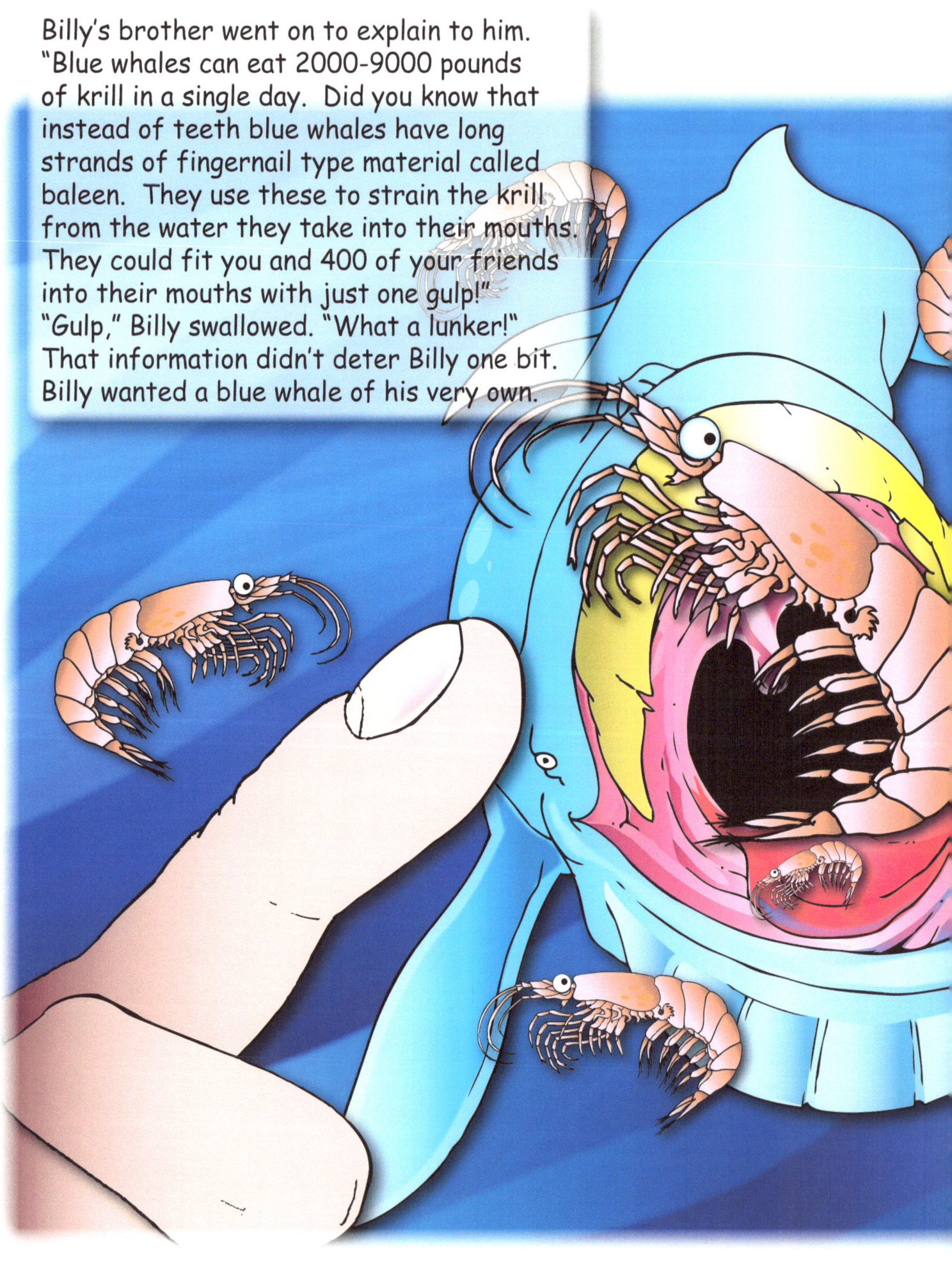

Billy's brother went on to explain to him. "Blue whales can eat 2000-9000 pounds of krill in a single day. Did you know that instead of teeth blue whales have long strands of fingernail type material called baleen. They use these to strain the krill from the water they take into their mouths. They could fit you and 400 of your friends into their mouths with just one gulp!"
"Gulp," Billy swallowed. "What a lunker!" That information didn't deter Billy one bit. Billy wanted a blue whale of his very own.

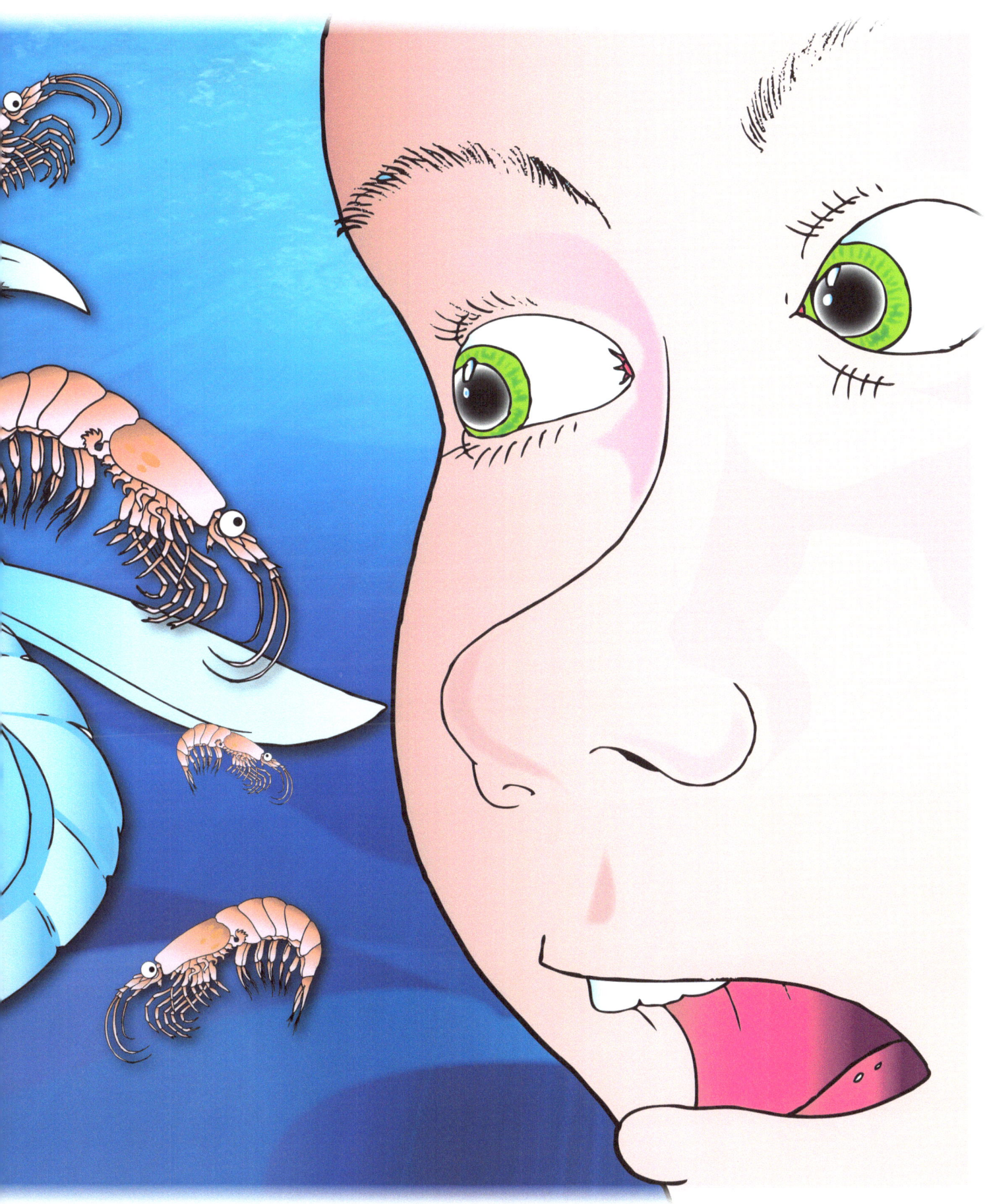

"Mommy, can I get a blue whale?" Billy asked his mother.
"I promise to take care of him."
"That sure would be nice Billy but where will you keep him?"
His mother asked.
"Maybe I could keep him in the pool?" Billy responded.
"In the pool? His mother sighed.
"He won't even fit in the back yard silly!"

"Adult blue whales can reach lengths of up to 100 feet!"
Billy's mother informed him. "That is longer than two school buses."
"A baby blue whale can measure up to 25 feet and weigh
a whopping 6000 pounds right out of his mommy's tummy!"
His mother went on to explain. "When you were born Billy you only
measured 19 inches and weighed around 9 pounds.
Blue whales are the largest animals to have ever lived!"
"Even bigger than dinosaurs?" Billy inquired.

"Blue whales are even bigger than a brontosaurus!"
His mother replied. Billy was amazed.
Brontosaurus was a marvelous creature.
Its name means "thunder lizard!"
That didn't change Billy's mind.
Now he wanted a blue whale more than ever...... but how?
He decided to ask the smartest person he knew.

Billy's Grandfather was a wise old fellow, with books on all sorts of topics. Surely his grandfather could help him. "Grandpa," Billy said "I want a blue whale, can you help me?" "My goodness." Billy's grandfather sounded puzzled. "That will be very difficult Billy. This book says there may not be many left in the wild. They were nearly hunted to extinction by whalers," explained his grandfather. "Why would anybody want to do something like that?" Billy wondered. Blue whales were far to magnificent to be treated in such a manner.

"Did you know Billy that a blue whale or Balaenoptera musculus can spout water 30 feet from the blow holes in the top of his head? That is taller than two giraffes or as high as a three story building!" His grandfather informed him. "Their tongues can weigh up to 3000 pounds, and their heart is the size of your mothers car." This was information overload for young Billy. He was starting to get the picture....Blue whales were very VERY big!

"When a blue whale sings, its song is louder than an airplane and can be heard from over 1000 miles away." Billy's grandfather concluded. Later that evening, Billy sat in his bedroom pondering. He could not seem to wrap his head around all the facts he had just learned.
Maybe blue whales really did only belong in the wild?
Billy imagined swimming next to the extraordinary creature.
"Wow" Billy thought to himself. "You would feel like a mouse!"

"Billy, come downstairs!" His father called out.
"There is somebody here who would like to meet you."
Billy jumped up, rushed out of his room and down the steps.
"A puppy!" Billy shouted with excitement.
"I've always wanted a puppy!"
"What are you going to name her Billy?" His father asked.

"I am going to name her Balaenoptera musculus."
Billy answered with delight.
"I will call her 'Bala' for short."
So let this be lesson to you all. Though some animals are truly amazing. They belong in the wild and may not make the best pet. Even though blue whales are one of the coolest animals on earth, a dog is a man's best friend.

This book belongs to: _____

About the author:
Hi there kids. My name is Cudd Fish.
I live in beautiful British Columbia Canada.
I started writing childrens books so that I could do something special for my son.
I have always wanted to write and illustrate a book and now I can finally say I have.
My advice to all you kids out there.
Dream big! But dont stop there.
You can accomplish anything you put your mind to.
It all starts with dream.
It is up to you to make your dream a reality.
So dream on!

www.cuddlefishbooks.com
Follow me on twitter
@Cudd_L_Fish
or like my books and find out what is up and coming
in the world of cuddlefish books
on facebook